A JOURNEY THROUGH THE EVOLUTION OF CHILDREN'S FASHION FROM 1920 TO TODAY

1920-1960: THE BEGINNINGS OF CHILDREN'S FASHION

The beginning of the 20th century marked a turning point in the evolution of children's fashion. While newborns were been swaddled in pieces of fabric for centuries, knitted clothing was devised in the 1920s.

1960-1970: THE SPIRIT OF HAUTE COUTURE

The cultural revolution of the 1960s revolutionized children's fashion. Younger children's wardrobes evolved as women's clothing evolved. This period marks the beginning of haute couture's interest in children's fashion.

1970-1990: THE DEMOCRATIZATION OF CHILDREN'S FASHION

The boom of the 1960s paved the way for the democratization of children's fashion. Starting in the 1970s, ready-to-wear brands specializing in children's clothing emerged. In the 1980s, sportswear brands exploded, Invading the world of clothing. Platform sneakers or high-tops, baseball caps or those with the colors of their favorite basketball team: the sportswear style also entered children's clothing market.

FROM 1990 TO THE PRESENT

Since 1990, children's fashion has acquired an unprecedented importance. Major brands have fully embraced the adventure, and haute couture is no longer reserved exclusively for adults. Children can now wear clothes identical to their parents', drawn from collections suitable for all ages. Parents make their dreams come true in their child's closet: princess dresses, dandy looks, elegant accessories—nothing is too beautiful for little ones. This demonstrates the status of children's fashion around the world, which continues to grow and evolve.

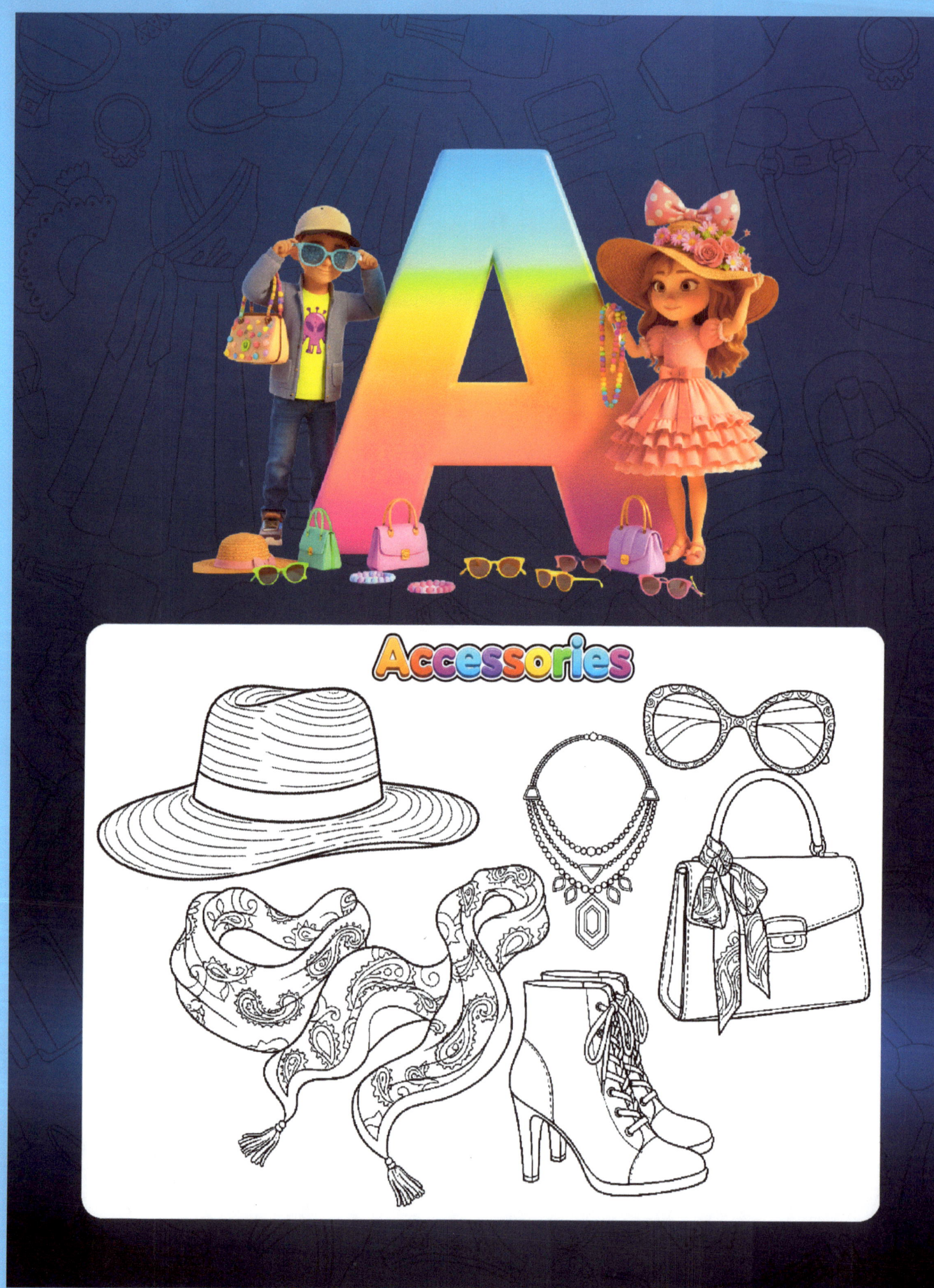

Couture

Hair Stylist

Fast Fashion

Leggings

Pullover

Style

Vintage

Counting Numbers 1-10

 Hat

 Bags

 Sunglasses

 Shoes

 Bracelets

 Watches

 Shirts

 Bows

 Stars

 Buttons

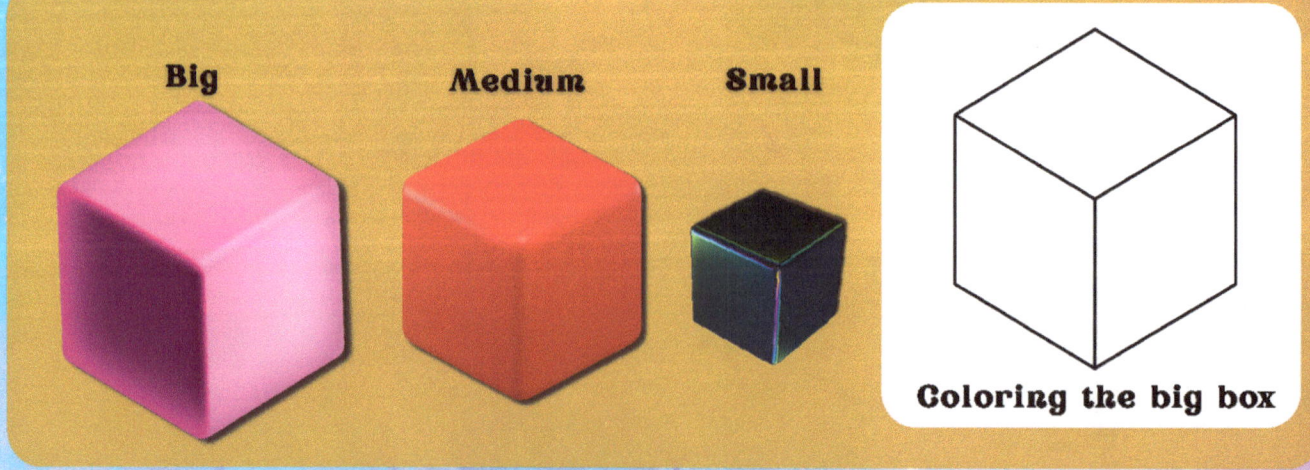

Big   Medium   Small

Coloring the big box

Fashion Game

Create your daily look

Collection Autumn/Winter

- T-shirt ☐
- Pullover ☐
- Hat ☐
- Jeans ☐
- Trench Coat ☐
- Jackets ☐
- Gloves ☐
- Watch ☐
- Cap ☐
- Bracelet ☐
- Scarf ☐
- Headphone ☐

Collection Spring/Summer

- Dress ☐
- Sandals ☐
- Flat ☐
- Bag ☐
- Hat ☐
- Shorts ☐
- T-shirt ☐
- Jeans ☐
- Utility Vest ☐
- Beach closes ☐
- Hand bag ☐
- Vest ☐

A/W Collection

Range of colors   Red Maroon Brown Green Blue Blue Sparkle Gold

Designer for One Day!

Challenge each other in a school contest under the banner of "passion for fashion" creating their own collection based on their ideals!

S. Alexander   **Will**   **RJ**   **Scarlet**   **Light**   **Blair**

S. Alexander

Will

RJ

Scarlet

Light

Blair